Peter de Jager's

The Bug Stops Here...!

A collection of both Humor and Hubris relating to the biggest, dumbest, most idiotic blunder in the history of technology...Known to one and all as

the Y2K Millennium Bug

A PARODY

The publisher disclaims all warranties with regards to Year 2000 compliance of the humor within this book. The publisher makes no warranties that the performance or functionality of said humor will be affected by dates prior to, during or after the Year 2000 or that the book will be capable of correctly processing, providing, and/or receiving dated humor within and between centuries, including the proper exchange of humorous information between compliant and non-compliant companies, organizations, and/or individuals. In other words, it's a parody. If it ain't funny, blame it on Y2K!

ISBN 0-9671745-0-3

Printed in Canada

Second Edition 1999

Acknowledgements

Concept: Peter de Jager, Dee Smith, Stan Taylor, Bonnie Bray, Susie Chase
Abused Copywriter: Dee Smith
Editor/Den Mother/Butt Kicker: Bonnie Bray, Bray Communications, Inc.
Design and Illustrations: Stan Taylor, Susie Chase, Gold Dust Graphics, Inc.
Research: Bonnie Bray, Susie Chase, Penny George
Production: Susie Chase, Stan Taylor
Insultant: Bonnie Bray
Copies, Hole Punching, More Copies and Hole Punching: Donnette Massey, Brooke Guillory,
Rebecca Chase, Diane Staser, Aaron Newitt
Stimulants: Coffee, Chocolate, Frapuccino, all forms of Sugar
More Editing: Donnette Massey, Bonnie Bray
Proof Reader: Kitten Taylor, Donnette Massey, Penny George
Mechanical Layout: Susie Chase, Brooke Guillory
Data Entry: Penny George, Brooke Guillory, Susie Chase
Moral Support - Front Line: Antoinette, Jason and Karl de Jager
Moral Support - Troops: Cristin Shoultz, Christopher and Douglas Chase, John Jussel, Melba Bray, Lois Monk
Depressants: Black Jack, Ativan, Budweiser
Computer Consultant and Hand Holder: Ed Craig
Courier: Glen Steady
Video Consultation: Michael Trufant
Interviewer Extraordinaire: John Spain
Musical Interlude: Cameron Guillory
Breakfast Food: Single Malt Scotch & Beignets
Catering: All Fast Food Restaurants Within 100 Miles
Motivation: Fame, Fortune & Comic Relief
Dumb Ideas: All
Thought Provocation: Charmin, Angel Soft
Equalizers: Prozac, Paxil, Tylenol, Sudafed, Aleve, Maalox, Alka Seltzer
People in the Great Beyond: Harriet and Theodore Schatz, Shirley Jussel, David M. Bray, Jr.
Virtual Presence: Tenagra Corp.
Zero Heroes: Robin Guenier, Phil Dodd, Leon Kappleman, Richard Bergeon
MIA: Bill Gates
Putting Up With Peter: All

Dedicated to
Murphy the Patron Saint
of all Projects

Humor is an affirmation of dignity,
a declaration of man's superiority to all that befalls him.
Romain Gary, Promise at Dawn

I've been working on the year 2000 problem for the last eight years. The goal was always to wake people up to a known and solvable problem. With the help of a great many people around the world, that goal was, to greater and lesser degrees, achieved.

At the very least, no literate person can claim ignorance of Y2K.

Have we avoided all the 'doomsday' scenarios? I believe so, but only time will tell. The good news is, we won't have to wait long to find out. In the meantime, we've time for some reflection.

Y2K is, without doubt, the biggest technological blunder we've managed to create for ourselves. If it were not so huge, so all encompassing, the comparisons to taking pictures with the lens cap on; to locking the keys in the car; to running to get on the wrong plane; to cutting an inch off a plank of wood and finding out it's still too short would be apparent to everyone.

The problem with Y2K as an object of humor, is that to laugh at it, is to knowingly laugh at ourselves... difficult at the best of times... but best practiced in difficult times.

In the past I was labeled a 'doom sayer' for delivering this simple 'gloomy' message; 'Fix this problem or suffer the consequences'... I think those days are behind me.

Now that we are working on fixing the problem, I'd like to earn a different title, that of 'gloom slayer'... Here's the first offering. Enjoy.

Peter de Jager
Brampton, Ontario
February 2, 1999

A computer lets you make more mistakes faster than any invention in human history - with the possible exception of handguns and tequila.

Mitch Ratliffe

Wally Chrimpshaw, bagboy at Carl's Super Save, was the first to suspect that there may be a problem with the date code chip in the store's pricing system.

As scarce as truth is,
the supply has always been
in excess of the demand.

Josh Billings

9

If a trainstation is where the train stops,
what's a workstation. . .?
Anonymous

History teaches us that men
and nations behave wisely
once they have exhausted
all other alternatives.
Abba Eban

If the human race
wants to go to hell in a basket,
technology can help it get there by jet.
Charles M. Allen

"10...9...8...3...5...6...7...4...1...2..."

Progress might have been all right once,
but it's gone on too long.
Ogden Nash

A Year-2000 compliant amusement park.

Is the FAA Y2K compliant yet?
I don't know.
It's up in the air. . .

"This is your captain speaking. We want to thank you for flying with us on this first day of the new millennium. And we were...uh...wondering ...is there a computer programmer on board?"

Bankruptcy is a legal proceeding
in which you put your money
in your pants pocket
and give your coat to your creditors.

Jeff Pesis

You're not working on the *Year 2000 Date Problem* because...

You're already in Chapter 11.

Hardware: the parts of the computer that can be kicked.

Jeff Pesis

Holly Jean – was somewhat surprised to realize that her blind date with Harley Lumpkin was not the worst bad date she would have in her life.

Be thankful we're not getting
all the government we're paying for.
Will Rogers

Government announces services to be uneffected by
the millennium bug.

> Indignation does no good
> unless it is backed with a
> club of sufficient size to
> awe the opposition.
>
> *Edgar Watson Howe*

Let the chips fail where they may.

Unknown

29

The Q & A Show #1

The public is wonderfully tolerant.
It forgives everything except genius.

Oscar Wilde

Directions: Take two and bury your head in the sand.

Time goes, you say?
Ah no! Time stays, we go.
Henry Austin Dobson

Tempting, isn't it?

Nothing is impossible
for the person who doesn't have to do it.
Weller's Law

How most CEO's
see programmers.

How most programmers
see CEO's.

Peter discovers just one more irritating little problem with those pesky date sensitive computer chips.

"For better or worse, in sickness and in health, in good times and in bad, Y2K compliant or not...."

Confusion now hath made his masterpiece!
Shakespeare's Macbeth

41

Milleium

Millennieum

Milinieum

Millennium

If all else fails,
at least we'll have the spelling down.

How the Romans solved the 2 digit Y2K problem.

Q: What do you call 200 lawyers
at the bottom of the sea?

A: A good start!

Q: What do you call 2000 lawyers
at the bottom of the sea
on January 1, 2000?

A: Justice!

45

Forgive us our digits,
as we forgive our digitors.

Matthew 6:12/sort of

"I'm sorry, but everything after January 1, 2000 is a complete blank."

"It can't be the light at the end of the tunnel.
The power grids went down months ago."

49

I am an optimist.
It does not seem too much use
being anything else.
Sir Winston Churchill

51

Too bad that all the people
who know how to run the country
are busy driving taxicabs and cutting hair.

George Burns

"Sir, he says he's here to help with the Y2K problem. He heard it was caused by a shortage of Rams."

Do we not all spend the greater part
of our lives under the shadow of an event
that has not yet come to pass.

Maurice Maeterlinck

Into every life a little Armageddon must fall.

He who desires, but acts not,
breeds pestilence.

William Blake

The Real Millennium Bugs.

Electric clocks reveal to you
precisely when your fuses blew.

Leonard Schiff

Peter gave everyone in the computer room quite a start when he inadvertently tripped over the power cord.

The Future of Advertising

Dairyman, Beau Vine, discovered the unfortunate results of not checking whether his automated milking system was ready for the new millennium.

What is research,
but a blind date with knowledge.
Will Henry

With the shut down of the computer regulated refrigerator system, the boys at the Atlanta Disease Control Center were having some difficulty controlling the dreaded Bogaloosa Virus.

Government is the only institution
that can take a valuable commodity
like paper and make it worthless
by applying ink.

Ludwig Van Moses

"Today the federal government unveiled an aggressive, bold new billion dollar plan to stamp out Y2K."

Computers can figure out all kinds
of problems, except the things
in the world that just don't add up.

James Magary

You will find that the truth is often unpopular and the contest between agreeable fancy and disagreeable fact is equal. For, in the vernacular, we Americans are suckers for good news.

Adlai Stevenson

Fun with the Survivalist Family.

To err is human,
to fix the damn thing divine.
With apologies to Alexander Pope

71

The Q & A Show #2

Experience is the name
everyone gives to their mistakes.
Lady Windermere's Fan

Fun things to do with power lines after January 1, 2000.

I try to take one day at a time,
but sometimes several days
attack me at once.
Ashleigh Brilliant

Whenever a man does a
thoroughly stupid thing,
it is always from
the noblest of motives.
Oscar Wilde

79

Best safety lies in fear.

Shakespeare's Hamlet

Computer wizkid and singles bar slug, Lance Smoldering, displays his new creation to protect your computer system from the dreaded Y2K bug.

Every year it takes less time
to fly across the Atlantic,
and more time to drive to the office.

Anonymous

If you want things to stay as they are,
things will have to change.

Giuseppe di Lampedusa

Pantsco CEO, Levi Wrangler, soon discovered that by not addressing the Y2K computer problem regarding his factories automated systems, he had placed himself and Pantsco's entire future in jeopardy.

A study of economics usually reveals that the best time to buy anything is last year.

Marty Allen

87

Our duty as men
is to proceed
as if limits to our ability
did not exist.
Teilhard de Chardin

Triage is a highly technical process skillfully administered
by experienced IT professionals.

The Nobel Prize for Medicine in the year 2000 will go to Isa Feelinopain, the former COBOL programmer and inventor of the Y2K vaccine. According to Isa, the vaccine doesn't solve the problem, but after you take it, you just don't give a damn.

Everytime the government attempts
to handle our affairs,
it costs more and the results are way worse
than if we had handled them ourselves.

Benjamin Constant

Actually, the Y2K problem has a very simple solution.

Bureaucracy is a giant mechanism operated by pygmies.

Honore' de Balzac

"At last report, government officials claimed to be on top of the problem."

Gifts are like hooks.
Martial

"I'm not sure, son, but I've heard stories that many years ago, long before any of us were born, they used to carry electricity. Whatever that was."

The difference between genius and stupidity
is that genius has its limits.

Anonymous

To all of you working on this problem:
"May the SOURCE be with you."

Waldo was convinced that a superior race of aliens would appear in the nick of time to solve his Y2K problem. Waldo was also convinced that his real name was Thaldor of Zircon.

The Future of Advertising

By not preparing for Y2K, Wall Street hot shot Howard Smoot discovered that it wasn't as easy to make a fast buck as it use to be.

In the world of mules there are no rules.

Ogden Nash

Q: How do you pronounce "00"?

A: "uh-oh."

The only thing to do with
good advice is to pass it on.
It is never of any use to oneself.
Oscar Wilde

Circa 2000 A.D.
Post COBOL Man cave art.

The danger from computers is not that they will eventually get as smart as men, but we will meanwhile agree to meet them halfway.

Bernard Avishai

After her computer crashed due to the Y2K bug, Letitia continued to stare blankly at the screen, thinking that it might be one of those magic eye things she had heard so much about. After staring for several days, she was pretty sure she could see a horsey and a ducky.

The bright side of Y2K:
When industry shuts down, the environment should
improve dramatically.

"The golden handcuffs weren't doing the trick."

It's not whether you win or lose,
but how you place the blame.
Anonymous

The stock market, always on the cutting edge of technology,
gears up for Y2K information crisis.

It is not true that life
is one damn thing after another -
it's one damn thing over and over.

Edna St. Vincent Millay

Time is the great teacher,
but unfortunately it kills all its pupils.

Hector Berlioz

A COBOL programmer's idea of a vacation.

Life would be infinitely happier
if we could only be born at the age of eighty
and gradually approach eighteen.
Mark Twain

You're not working on the *Year 2000 Date Problem* because...

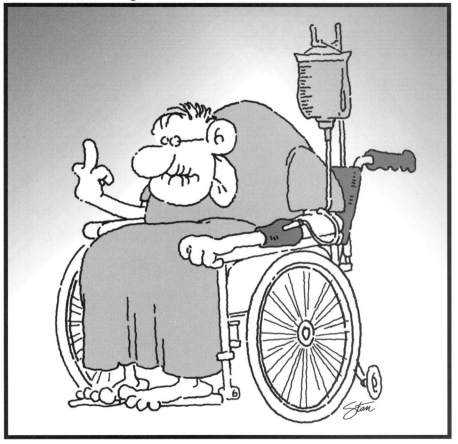

You're 95, on life support and haven't paid your electric bill
for the last three months.

The pessimist sees the difficulty
in every opportunity;
the optimist, the opportunity
in every difficulty.
L. P. Jacks

123

The Q & A Show #3

125

It is always with the best of intentions that the worst work is done.

Oscar Wilde

A carefully managed triage program is the heart
of every successful Y2K remediation effort.

Everyone is in a panic about Y2K.
I have a feeling that the first millennium was
not as big a deal. Around the year 998 AD,
all the computer geeks got together: "Oh, my
God... We are going to need more beads!"

"Leap year, schmeep year. 365 is close enough."

I should be angry with you,
if the time were convenient.

Shakespeare's Henry V

"Leave it up to Computer Programmers to abbreviate 'Year 2000' as 'Y2K'. Isn't that what got us this problem in the first place?"

133

The best brewer sometimes makes bad beer.

German Proverb

136

137

We are all in this together - by ourselves.

Lily Tomlin

Formal letter of Y2K compliance from software company.

Fun with the Survivalist Family; a Low-Cal cuisine 2000.

The year 2000 will see the birth of an entirely new post-Y2K programming language.

Nothing is more dangerous
than an idea,
When it is the only idea we have.
Alain

143

American Bandstand 2000.

A CEO's idea of Heaven.

A COBOL programmer's idea of Heaven.

Newly appointed Y2K projects manager, Ellis Ewe, was also
a first time Bungie jumper.

It is so pleasant to come across people
more stupid than ourselves.
We love them at once for being so.
Jerome K. Jerome

Nostradamas never mentioned it.

When we remember that we are all mad,
the mysteries disappear
and life stands explained.

Mark Twain

Y2K Programmer's Checklist

The trouble with the rat race is that even
if you win, you're still a rat.
Lily Tomlin

153

Death is a delightful hiding-place
for weary men.

Herodotus

Good news! Waldo spots his name in the obituaries
which means he doesn't have to put in another 15-hour day
as a COBOL programmer!

No one is entirely useless.
Even the worst of us
can serve as horrible examples.

Anonymous prisoner (State Prison, Salt Lake City)

157

When you get there,
there isn't any there there.

Gertrude Stein

There are days when it takes all you've got
just to keep up with the losers.

Robert Orpen

If this reminds you of your company's plan to eliminate the Y2K bug,
you'd better polish up the old resume.

There ain't no answer.
There ain't gonna be any answer.
There never has been an answer.
That's the answer.

Gertrude Stein

163

164

165

Rarely have so many people
been so wrong about so much.
Richard M. Nixon

167

Everything is improbable until
it moves into the past tense.
With apologies to George Ade

171

Results! Why, man, I have gotten a lot of results. I know several thousand things that won't work.
Thomas A. Edison

The Survivalist Family Microwave 2000

"Thou shalt not use two-digit date codes!"

175

Q: Why do some people spell it millennium and some people spell it millenium?

A: Some people are trying to save space.

More of your conversation
would infect my brain.
Shakespeare's Coriolanus

179

"Whose turn is it anyway?"

Don't Worry, Be Happy!
Bobby McFerrin

Rush Hour Traffic Monday, January 3, 2000.

When three people call you an ass, put on a bridle.

Spanish Proverb

185

Folly loves the martyrdom of fame.

Byron

In three words I can sum up everything
I've learned about life.
It goes on.
Robert Frost

Winners of the Digital Deflections and Diversions Contest

In Late 1998 I decided that Y2K was in need of a giggle. I held a Humor Contest
on www.year2000.com and offered some donations to charity as prizes.
Here are the winners.

First Prize Winner Submitted by: Ralph Lante
Prize money of $2,500 was donated to: Adelaide Children's Hospital Children's Burn Unit;
South Australia, Australia

St. Peter was at the Pearly gates processing some new arrivals after the Year 2000 meltdown. "So why should I let you in?" St. Peter asked the first man.

"I was the CEO of a large company. My efforts in raising Year 2000 awareness, fighting for budget approval and becoming personally involved in our compliance project almost saved the company from certain collapse. My dedication to the cause is documented in the many reports that..."

"Ok, ok that's enough, You can go in." St. Peter said.

A second man approached. "And why should you enter the Pearly gates?"

"I was a Year 2000 consultant. I dedicated the last year of my life working long hours to solve computer problems. My only motivation was a desire to see us through these difficult times, to stamp out this diabolical problem and to make sure we all..."

"That will do!" St. Peter called, "Make you way through the gate please."

"Now why should I let you in?" St. Peter said to the next person.

"I am a lawyer. I hovered over the scraps of society that were left after year 2000 and then swooped down like a bloodsucking vulture to pick the bones of any defenseless survivors that managed to survive the apocalypse. My only desire was to accumulate as much cash as possible."

"Hmmm", St. Peter thought about this for a while, "Ok you can go in."

An angel watching all this from above flew over to St Peter. "Hey what did you let him in for?" he asked.

St. Peter looked up. "We need to let a few of the honest ones get through too you know."

Second Prize Winner Submitted by: Chas Snyder
Prize money of $1,000 was donated to: Lifeline Women's Shelter; San Francisco, CA

If you own a clock that counts down, you might be a remediator.

If you think 'aging data for future regression tests' makes sense, you might be a remediator.

If you think Viagra is a software tool for fixing non-performing code, you might be a remediator.

If your spouse wants you to consider therapy because you tell everyone you play all day with time machines, you might be a remediator.

If you're at a dance and they play YMCA and you go Y2K ('Y' with your arms, '2' show 2 fingers, 'K' both arms out at the side), you might be a remediator.

If your mother thinks you are having a sexual identity crisis because you tell her you're always changing dates, you might be a remediator.

If you've looked at your family tree and caught yourself making test cases for each branch, you might be a remediator.

If you would rather see an investigator from Kenneth Starr's office show up at your desk than a Y2K PMO Manager, you might be a remediator.

If you have ever washed your child's mouth out with soap for saying the words 'Y2K Director' at the dinner table, you're certainly a remediator.

Second Prize Winner Submitted by: Patrick Angel
Prize money of $1,000 was donated to: KERA/Channel 13 (PBS); Dallas, Texas

Three Monkeys

One day this guy was walking down the street at lunch when he saw a Pet Store that had a big SALE sign in their window. Intrigued, he went inside to check it out. They had the usual - birds, dogs, cats, fish, etc. But the one that caught his eye was these three monkeys in their cages showcased in the middle of the floor. He went up to the counter and asked about them.

"What's the deal with the monkeys?" he inquired. The owner came up and said "Ahh, you've got a good eye. They are each very special - let's start with the first one." The monkey sat quietly, picking at his fur, brushing himself and cleaning up his cage and seemed happy at the attention.

"This monkey is very talented - he can handle your office duties. He knows word processing, spreadsheets, can bang out presentations in no time and is very organized - his filing is amazing."

"Wow, I had no idea," replies the customer, "How much is it?"

"This one is $300."

"What about the others?" The customer asked. They moved onto the second monkey which seemed just a little quirky - he'd move from side to side and was a little fidgety with lots of candy bar wrappers at the bottom of the cage.

"They all have special talents. Let me show you the next one. This monkey here is amazingly proficient in computers and programming. He can build databases, design web pages in JAVA, and HTML. He knows all about networks and can bring your whole office up to the 21st century in technology."

"Jesus, that's amazing! How much is THIS monkey?" Asked the customer. "This one is a pretty good deal at $1,000." Having his attention piqued, the customer wanted to know more.

"Okay, what about the last monkey. How much is this one worth?" The third monkey looked back at them and turned away disinterested.

"Ahhh... this is the most expensive monkey here. This monkey is $5,000."

"Sheesh" replied the customer, "I bet this one can do everything huh?!"

"Well, actually," said the owner, "this monkey is always doing something and looks busy, but he never really produces anything. He's a Y2K Consultant Monkey."

Third Prize Winner Submitted by: Martin Rene
Prize money of $500 was donated to: "Les enfants de l'espoir" (children of hope);
Montréal, Québec, Canada

1-800-SUE-4Y2K
Welcome to The Day After, Inc.
Please select one of the following:
To file a lawsuit pertaining to Y2K; press 1.
For litigations related to Y2K; press 2.
To obtain legal counseling on Y2K; press 3.
For suing back a Y2K lawsuit; press 4.
For Y2K claims and warranties; press 5.
To retrace a Y2K contractor; press 6.
To know the status of your Y2K lawsuit, press 7.
To obtain our brochure "A date with money"; press 8.
< 7 pressed> dial tone.

Third Prize Winner Submitted by: Juan Gaspar
Prize money of $500 was donated to: CARITAS ESPAÑOLAS; Madrid, Spain

I don't know what Y2K effect is, but I'll change my hardware, my software and
my underwear, just in case. Happy New Year!

Third Prize Winner Submitted by: Leonard Cifelli
Prize money of $500 was donated to: The Santa Clarita Valley Food Pantry; Newhall, CA

What is the difference between a Y2K planner and a terrorist?
You can negotiate with a terrorist.

My thanks to all who participated. I wish you all a Happy New Year!
P. de Jager

For more information on the Year 2000 Computer Crisis: www.year2000.com
To contact Peter de Jager for Speaking Engagements: bookings@year2000.com
or contact:
Exclusive Worldwide Representative:

        Bray Communications, Incorporated
        6719 Perkins Road
        Baton Rouge, Louisiana 70808-4263
        Email: info@braycom.com
        Telephone: (225) 767-8600
        Fax: (225) 767-8661

Additional copies may be ordered: www.year2000.com, cartoon.book@year2000.com
or 1-877-Y2K-JOKE, 1-877-925-5653 (US and Canada)